31 Days of Encouragement
1 Day at a Time

SAM Morrison

Other Books by SAM Morrison

Shining Light into the Darkness
Praying the Word over your Wounds
Intentional Acts of Loving-Kindness
A Year of Thankfulness
Legacy
A Year of Proverbs
Fuel your Body
Prayer Journal
A Pondering Place – The Original
A Pondering Place – Scripture Version
A Pondering Place – Business Version
A Pondering Place – Recovery Version
Sweet Baby

ISBN-13:978-1717023681
ISBN-10:1717023681

All Scriptures NIV

In each of my book projects I take a small space to thank the people in my life that love me. My list is long. Very long. Somehow saying thank you is not enough so instead of saying thank you this time I will say that I promise to do my best to live the life that God has created me to live and leave a legacy of love worthy of being remembered.

Peace and grace to all,

SAM

"Never forget what Jesus did for you. Never take lightly what it cost Him. And never assume that if it cost Him His very life, that it wont also cost you yours". Rich Mullins

If an encouragement comment does not have an author listed, it was written by SAM.

Who is SAM?

My name is SAM. I have struggled with a weight issue most of my adult life. I have spent a lot of time and energy on healing from many different things that have happened in my life and have come to understand that most of the choices I have made, including those about food, have been due to **low self-worth**.

By addressing my self-worth issue, I have been able to see healing in many areas of my life and am now ready to focus on my food choices.

This book is for me as much as it is for you. I have heard it said that we usually teach on what we need to learn ourselves.

I am not a food, health or weight loss expert but I am a Christian that loves Jesus and believes that when we turn to Him and live our life one day at a time, He will guide us and we can overcome the issues in our life.

I am part of Celebrate Recovery and when I share my testimony the verse that I typically open with is: I appeal to you therefore, brothers, by the mercies of God, to present your bodies as a living sacrifice, holy and acceptable to God, which is your spiritual worship. Romans 12:1 ESV

May we allow our bodies to truly be holy and acceptable to God today and always by how we live our lives every day.

Blessings,

SAM

How to Use this Book

You can start on day one and go through the book one day at a time or you can start on today's date, meaning that if today is the 10th of the month, you would start on day 10 and move forward from there.

I can almost guarantee that if you go through this book for 31 days and then do it a 2nd or even 3rd time God will show you something different each time. I believe God shows us things when we are ready to know them. Depending on where you are in your life a certain encouraging thought or scripture will speak to you in different ways.

I believe in the power of writing. Please take the time to write down your thoughts and prayers each day so that you can have them to look back on over time and see the progress you have made and the answered prayers.

You may notice that I don't actually talk a lot about food or exercise in this book. That is on purpose. I don't think that the food or lack of exercise is the issue. Connecting more with God and finding your worth in Christ and who He created you to be will allow some of the unhealthy choices to fall away.

This book could be used as encouragement for anyone trying to make a different choice in any area of their life, not just someone dealing with food/health issues.

As you work through this book, more than anything, I want you to realize that there is hope in every area of life.

Blessings to you today and forever.

Day 1

Encouragement
Giving up on your goal because of one set back is like slashing your other three tires because you have one flat tire. Author Unknown

Thoughts
I have come to understand that even when I fail, as long as I don't give up I will continue to make progress towards my goal.   At any moment you can make a new decision and work towards your goal again. Just don't give up. What God is teaching you through your challenge will be a blessing. I know this because His Word says it is.

Scripture
Consider it pure joy, my brothers and sisters, whenever you face trials of many kinds, because you know that the testing of your faith produces perseverance. Let perseverance finish its work so that you may be mature and complete, not lacking anything. James 1:2-4

Day 1

Day 2

Encouragement
When God pushes you to the edge, trust Him fully, because only one of two things will happen. Either He will catch you when you fall or He will teach you to fly. Author Unknown

Thoughts
When was the last time you stepped out on faith? Really trusted God? I would like to encourage you to pray and listen for God to guide you to the place where you only depend on Him. When you realize that God is all you have and understand that He is all you really need, your life will change. You will see God show up in your life in some amazing ways.

Scripture
Blessed are the pure in heart, for they will see God. Matthew 5:8

Day 2

_____

_____

_____

_____

_____

_____

_____

_____

_____

_____

_____

_____

_____

_____

_____

_____

_____

Day 3

Encouragement

The first step to getting what you want is having the courage to get rid of what you do not want.
Author Unknown

Thoughts

If you are like me you know what area(s) of your life that you need to take steps to improve. You don't even have to think about it. You know what you need to get rid of but for some reason it is harder than just making the decision. I pray that you will find your strength in Jesus. Focus on Him and His truth and know that because of His love and grace you can break any stronghold.

Scripture

Therefore, with minds that are alert and fully sober, set your hope on the grace to be brought to you when Jesus Christ is revealed at his coming.
1 Peter 1:3

Day 3

_____

_____

_____

_____

_____

_____

_____

_____

_____

_____

_____

_____

_____

_____

_____

_____

_____

Day 4

Encouragement
Sometimes you win. Sometimes you learn.
John C. Maxwell

Thoughts
Even when you don't reach your goal if you really think about the situation you will have an opportunity to learn something. Trust that God is your strength and He will help you learn how to move forward, even when you don't win.

Scripture
Surely God is my salvation; I will trust and not be afraid. The LORD, is my strength and my song; he has become by salvation. Isaiah 12:2

Day 4

_____

_____

_____

_____

_____

_____

_____

_____

_____

_____

_____

_____

_____

_____

_____

_____

_____

Day 5

Encouragement
Some people dream of success, others make it happen. Author Unknown

Thoughts
Father – I pray that you touch the heart of every person reading this book to give them peace and understanding that they can reach their healthy weight or overcome any stronghold in their life. Please allow them to rest in the grace, peace and forgiveness of your love that is never-ending. Amen.

Scripture
Peace I leave with you; my peace I give you. I do not give to you as the world gives. Do not let your hearts be troubled and do not be afraid.
John 14:27

Day 5

_____

_____

_____

_____

_____

_____

_____

_____

_____

_____

_____

_____

_____

_____

_____

_____

_____

Day 6

Encouragement
Simply your life.
Author Unknown

Thoughts
As I look around my life I realize it is surrounded by so much to do. Being busy in some ways brings me comfort. In the past I believed that if I was "too busy" to cook healthy foods or to workout, then it was not my fault that I was not taking care of my body. But now I understand that is just an excuse and that I get to choose everything I do. Find ways to simply your life. It is okay to say no to some things so that you can say yes to taking care of yourself. If you let him, God will guide you.

Scripture
Finally, be strong in the Lord and in His mighty power. Ephesians 6:10

Day 6

_____

_____

_____

_____

_____

_____

_____

_____

_____

_____

_____

_____

_____

_____

_____

_____

Day 7

Encouragement
Kids do not make up 100% of our population but they do make up 100% of our future.
Zig Ziglar

Thoughts
Our kids need to learn how to eat healthy. Just imagine how different their lives could be if food was something that they used to fuel their body and not comfort their hurts. As you learn how to take your health back please be sure to pay it forward to someone else, especially someone younger than you. You may not be a parent but you can bless a child by stepping in and helping them in this way. This could change the course of their life and possibly even extend their life.

Scripture
Start children off on the way they should go, and even when they are old they will not turn from it.
Proverbs 22:6

Day 7

_____

_____

_____

_____

_____

_____

_____

_____

_____

_____

_____

_____

_____

_____

_____

_____

_____

Day 8

Encouragement
Action always beats intention.
Jon Acuff

Thoughts
Jesus – I pray that we would have the faith of Noah to build what you have called us to build in our life even when no one else understands. I ask that you give us the strength to do what needs to be done and that all the glory for our success will go to You and You alone. I pray that we will be people of prayer and action. Thank you for loving us and showing us your mercy and grace. Amen.

Scripture
But Noah found favor in the eyes of the Lord.
Genesis 6:8

Day 8

_____

_____

_____

_____

_____

_____

_____

_____

_____

_____

_____

_____

_____

_____

Day 9

Encouragement
The two most important days in your life are the day you were born and the day you find out why.
Mark Twain

Thoughts
What were you born to do? I have been struggling with my weight almost all my life. I can tell you for sure, that struggling with my weight is NOT what God called me to do. Find your way regarding your food choices and healthy lifestyle so that you can focus your time and energy on being who Jesus created you to be. Do not be surprised if you realize that God is going to use the biggest mess in your life to share His love with others. My mess has become His message of grace, mercy and forgiveness to the world.

Scripture
But the angel said to her, "Do not be afraid, Mary; you have found favor with the Lord. Luke 1:30

Day 9

_____

_____

_____

_____

_____

_____

_____

_____

_____

_____

_____

_____

_____

_____

_____

_____

_____

_____

Day 10

Encouragement
The greatest pleasure in life is doing what people say you cannot do. Walter Bagehot

Thoughts
Have you been told you are not good enough? That you will never be able to accomplish your dreams? Well, me too. Here is the thing, those are just lies from the devil. Focus on living the life that you know God has called you to and you will be fulfilled beyond measure and you will have the pleasure of proving all those liars wrong!

Scripture
Hope deferred makes the heart sick; but a longing fulfilled is a tree of life. Proverbs 13:12

Day 10

_____

_____

_____

_____

_____

_____

_____

_____

_____

_____

_____

_____

_____

_____

_____

_____

_____

_____

Day 11

Encouragement
Do not look back – you are not going that way.
Author Unknown

Thoughts
Focus on your future and having the life that God called you to. Learn from your past but do not live there.

Scripture
Joshua said to them, "Do not be afraid; do not be discouraged. Be strong and courageous.
Joshua 10:25

Day 11

_____

_____

_____

_____

_____

_____

_____

_____

_____

_____

_____

_____

_____

_____

_____

_____

_____

Day 12

Encouragement
Did you drink enough water yesterday?

Thoughts
Just like your physical body needs water your spiritual body needs the Living Water that only comes from Jesus. Be sure to spend time with Jesus every day. He will give you what you need to make it through your day. When you start your day with the Lord and rest in His grace you will see things in a whole new light.

Scripture
But whoever drinks the water I give them will never thirst. Indeed, the water I give them will become in them a spring of water welling up to eternal life. John 4:14

Day 12

_____

_____

_____

_____

_____

_____

_____

_____

_____

_____

_____

_____

_____

_____

_____

_____

Day 13

Encouragement
You are not in the same place of the journey as anyone else so don't judge yourself based on how far they are ahead of you or behind you. Your only competition is you.

Thoughts
Remember God is not done with you yet. He is molding you to be the person that He created you to be. Be sure to give that same understanding to others around you. There is enough grace for everyone. Thank you, Jesus, for that truth.

Scripture
Trust in the LORD with all your heart and lean not on your own understanding; in all your ways acknowledge him, and he will make your paths straight.   Proverbs 3:5-6

Day 13

Day 14

Encouragement
Do what you love. Love what you do.
Author Unknown

Thoughts
Father – thank you for today. Thank you for being my refuge and shield. Keep me focused on you and what you would have me do today. I love you and want to give you praise for all that you have done for me. Amen.

Scripture
You are my refuge and my shield; I have put my hope in your word. Away from me, you evildoers, that I may keep the commands of my God!
Psalm 119:114-115

Day 14

_____

_____

_____

_____

_____

_____

_____

_____

_____

_____

_____

_____

_____

_____

_____

_____

Day 15

Encouragement
We were loved, forgiven and set free.
The order matters.

Thoughts
Do you really believe Jeremiah 29:11? If you do
your life will show it. My prayer for you (and me)
today is that we would believe that God's word
really is true and that He has a plan for us.

Scripture
For I know the plans I have for you, declares the
LORD, plans to prosper you and not to harm you,
plans to give you hope and a future.
Jeremiah 29:11

Day 15

_____

_____

_____

_____

_____

_____

_____

_____

_____

_____

_____

_____

_____

_____

_____

_____

Day 16

Encouragement
If you want to be happy – start with you. It always starts with you. A relationship, job or other situation will not make you happy if you aren't happy to begin with.

Thoughts
Some days life is just hard. Really hard. There is no other way to describe it. If we make turning to God every day part of our life then it will be natural on the hard days to turn to Him. Happiness is a choice. Even when things seem bleak you can choose to find the silver lining.

Scripture
Let us then approach God's throne of grace with confidence, so that we may receive mercy and find grace to help us in our time of need. Hebrews 4:6

Day 16

_____

_____

_____

_____

_____

_____

_____

_____

_____

_____

_____

_____

_____

_____

_____

_____

_____

Day 17

Encouragement
God is always with us. Every conversation. Every meal. Everything we do in private, he is there. Be thankful for that today.

Thoughts
Father – give us the words to share your love with everyone we come in contact with, even ourselves. Sometimes we do a better job of taking care of others than we do ourselves. Please help us replace the lies we tell ourselves with the Truth of your word and allow us to believe those truths.

Scripture
Let your conversation be always full of grace; seasoned with salt, so that you may know how to answer everyone. Colossians 4:6

Day 17

_____

_____

_____

_____

_____

_____

_____

_____

_____

_____

_____

_____

_____

_____

_____

_____

_____

Day 18

Encouragement
Obstacles cannot stop you. Problems cannot stop you. Most of all other people cannot stop you. The only one who stops you is you. J. Gitomer

Thoughts
Belief is a powerful thing. If you believe you can, you are right. If you believe you cannot, you are also right. That's a paraphrase from Henry Ford. Believe that you can reach your goals. Believe that you can make different choices. Believe that you are who God says you are.

Scripture
I can do all things through Him who gives me strength. Philippians 4:13

Day 18

_____

_____

_____

_____

_____

_____

_____

_____

_____

_____

_____

_____

_____

_____

_____

_____

Day 19

Encouragement
While reaching for something new and better do not forget to be thankful for what you have.

Thoughts
Do you remember that old school church song; Count your blessings, name them one by one? I think about that when I focus on what I want while being reminded of what I already have. Having a goal and a plan to get where you need to be is a good thing. Just be sure to be thankful for what you already have and help others along the way. You can encourage someone today. Share your hope for the future with a friend that needs it. By focusing on helping others you will be more blessed than you can imagine.

Scripture
Greater love has no one than this; to lay down one's life for one's friends. John 15:13

Day 19

_____

_____

_____

_____

_____

_____

_____

_____

_____

_____

_____

_____

_____

_____

_____

_____

_____

Day 20

Encouragement
The only people that can stop me are me, myself and I. We have talked. They are on board so its all good. Author Unknown

Thoughts
Jesus – today may we be reminded that we are yours not because of anything we have done but because of your gift of grace, love and mercy. Please allow us to focus on making the next right choice not because of some idea of duty but out of true love for you and the understanding that all we have is yours. We love you and want to honor you with all our life. Amen.

Scripture
For sin shall no longer be your master, because you are not under the law, but under grace.
Romans 6:14

Day 20

_____

_____

_____

_____

_____

_____

_____

_____

_____

_____

_____

_____

_____

_____

_____

_____

_____

_____

Day 21

Encouragement
Your hardest times often lead to the greatest moments in your life. Keep the faith. It will all be worth it in the end. Lifelifehappy.com

Thoughts
Today we need to remember that God really does have a plan for us. Many times, His plans do not make sense to us. But because He can see our life from beginning to end and we know that His love for us is bigger than we can even comprehend we can decide to have faith in Him. Rest in Him. Trust in Him and believe it will all be okay, eventually.

Scripture
Cast all your anxiety on him because he cares for you. 1 Peter 5:7

Day 21

_____

_____

_____

_____

_____

_____

_____

_____

_____

_____

_____

_____

_____

_____

_____

_____

Day 22

Encouragement
Jesus.

Thoughts
Jesus. The only name that saves. Jesus said that the most important thing was to love the Lord your God and others as yourself. Does your life reflect that? We should be different because of His love for us. Today spend some time with Jesus to deepen your love for Him. It will change you when you love him with all your soul, mind and strength.

Scripture
Love the Lord your God with all your heart and all your soul and with all your mind and with all of your strength. Mark 12:30

Day 21

_____

_____

_____

_____

_____

_____

_____

_____

_____

_____

_____

_____

_____

_____

_____

_____

Day 22

Encouragement
Jesus.

Thoughts
Jesus. The only name that saves. Jesus said that the most important thing was to love the Lord your God and others as yourself. Does your life reflect that? We should be different because of His love for us. Today spend some time with Jesus to deepen your love for Him. It will change you when you love him with all your soul, mind and strength.

Scripture
Love the Lord your God with all your heart and all your soul and with all your mind and with all of your strength. Mark 12:30

Day 22

_____

_____

_____

_____

_____

_____

_____

_____

_____

_____

_____

_____

_____

_____

_____

Day 23

Encouragement
Be who God created you to be.

Thoughts
God created you. God loves you. God will provide for you. If you have accepted His love and have called on Him to be your savior, then you are a winner. His power is at work in you. Give Him praise today for all that he has done for you and all that He will do in the future. Do not give up on yourself. He has not given up on you and He wont. Ever.

Scripture
Now to him who is able to do immeasurably more than all we ask or imagine, according to his power that is at work within us, to Him be glory in the church and in Christ Jesus throughout all generations, for ever and ever! Amen.
Ephesians 3:20-21

Day 23

_____

_____

_____

_____

_____

_____

_____

_____

_____

_____

_____

_____

_____

_____

_____

_____

Day 24

Encouragement
Light shines best through broken things.

Thoughts
Father – we love you and worship you for who you are. Thank you for saving us and for calling us your own. Please give us strength to remember that even though we struggle we are still secure in you. Thank you for loving us and giving us the ability to continue on our path. We are thankful that you use broken things and that even though we are broken we can be made whole and complete in you. Amen.

Scripture
For it is by grace you have been saved, through faith – and this is not from yourselves, it is the gift of God. Ephesians 2:8

Day 24

Day 25

Encouragement
If it has ingredients it is not food.
Author Unknown

Thoughts
Today as you decide what to fuel your body with consider eating less processed foods. If you cannot pronounce the words on the ingredient label it is really not food but a chemical. If you can start choosing more real food you will start to feel better and your body will thank you for it.

Scripture
Taste and see that the Lord is good; blessed is the one who takes refuge in him. Psalm 34:8

Day 25

_____

_____

_____

_____

_____

_____

_____

_____

_____

_____

_____

_____

_____

_____

_____

_____

_____

Day 26

Encouragement
We are better together. Life was meant to be lived in relationship with God and with each other.

Thoughts
God created us to be in community. However, many of us have been hurt by trusting people in the past. May I suggest to you: trust anyway. We are stronger together than we are alone. Find a few close friends that you can do life with and share your joys and sorrows. Having a good group of people that you can be real with will bless your soul and theirs.

Scripture
As iron sharpens iron, so one person sharpens another. Proverbs 27:17

Day 26

_____

_____

_____

_____

_____

_____

_____

_____

_____

_____

_____

_____

_____

_____

_____

_____

_____

Day 27

Encouragement
Every accomplishment starts with the decision to try. Gail Devers

Thoughts
Father – thank you for everything you have given us. We praise you today and forever. We are on a journey to a better relationship with you, people in our life and our health. We have decided to break the strongholds in our life. We ask you today to renew our strength and commitment to honor you with everything we do. Amen.

Scripture
But those who hope in the Lord will renew their strength. They will soar on wings like eagles; they will run and not grow weary, they will walk and not be faint. Isaiah 40:31

Day 27

_____

_____

_____

_____

_____

_____

_____

_____

_____

_____

_____

_____

_____

_____

_____

Day 28

Encouragement
Question what you believe to be true because everything else flows from that.

Thoughts
Our thoughts are one of the most important things we need to manage. What we believe controls our thoughts. Our thoughts control our actions. When we believe that God is with us and we trust that His word is true our lives can be different.

Scripture
In everything he did he had great success, because the Lord was with him. 1 Samuel 18:14

Day 28

_____

_____

_____

_____

_____

_____

_____

_____

_____

_____

_____

_____

_____

_____

_____

_____

Day 29

Encouragement
Those who leave everything in God's hands will eventually see God's hands in everything.
Quotediary.me

Thoughts
Waiting for the "eventually" is difficult; I know that and am sure you do too. I find it odd that we call ourselves "believers" when many times we aren't. I am thankful that Jesus understands that we believe but need help with our unbelief. Put your faith in Jesus and He will never let you down. Trust Him to guide your steps. Pray and ask Him to show you the way. Believe that He will and you will have ears to listen and eyes to see. Then you will have to be willing to walk in the light of the Truth that He has shown you.

Scripture
The Lord delights in those who fear him, who put their hope in his unfailing love. Psalm 147:11

Day 29

_____

_____

_____

_____

_____

_____

_____

_____

_____

_____

_____

_____

_____

_____

_____

_____

_____

_____

Day 30

Encouragement
Success in life is the result of good judgment.
Good judgment is usually the result of experience.
Experience is usually the result of bad judgement.
Anthony Robbins

Thoughts
Mistakes are a part of life. Use those mistakes to help you learn and grow. One thing is true above all else – you are loved exactly as you are. Give yourself some grace and know that just because you have made some bad choices you don't have to continue down that destructive path. Today is a new day. Focus on how truly loved you are and I believe your choices can change.

Scripture
We love because he first loved us. 1 John 4:19

Day 30

_____

_____

_____

_____

_____

_____

_____

_____

_____

_____

_____

_____

_____

_____

_____

_____

Day 31

Encouragement
Enjoy the process. The process is called LIFE!

Thoughts
You have probably heard it said before that the joy is in the journey not the destination. I agree with that but only on this side of heaven. We have been promised eternal life through Christ. This should give us such joy today and every day that we live our life differently than those that do not have this promise. Enjoy your life. Be happy. Be complete in Jesus and share His love with others.

Scripture
And this is what He promised to us eternal life.
1 John 2:25

Day 31

_____

_____

_____

_____

_____

_____

_____

_____

_____

_____

_____

_____

_____

_____

_____

_____

Use the following pages to continue to journal.

Made in the USA
San Bernardino, CA
21 June 2018